Parched Paper

A Tapestry of Words

Kasturi Ghosh

ARCHWAY PUBLISHING

Archway Publishing books may be ordered
through booksellers or by contacting:

Archway Publishing
1663 Liberty Drive
Bloomington, IN 47403
www.archwaypublishing.com
1 (888) 242-5904

Because of the dynamic nature of the Internet, any web
addresses or links contained in this book may have changed
since publication and may no longer be valid. The views
expressed in this work are solely those of the author and do
not necessarily reflect the views of the publisher, and the
publisher hereby disclaims any responsibility for them.

Any people depicted in stock imagery provided
by Getty Images are models, and such images are
being used for illustrative purposes only.
Certain stock imagery © Getty Images.

ISBN: 978-1-4808-6864-9 (sc)
ISBN: 978-1-4808-6865-6 (e)

Library of Congress Control Number: 2018911210

Print information available on the last page.

Archway Publishing rev. date: 9/28/2018

It's only words, and words are all I have

To take your heart away.....BeeGees

Contents

Acknowledgements

To Baba, Ma and Biks for watering my words,
To Sal for a love that goes beyond words.

To Baba...my cheerleader, guide, friend and joy
The fire in my belly,
The iron in my spine,
I got from you dad.
You built me to shine.

The words in my poems,
The dreams in my mind,
I borrowed from you dad.
You said seek n you shall find.

The laughter in my days,
The mischief in my eye,
You gave to me dad.
Saying girls needn't be shy.

The pride in my job,
The wings in my boots,
Its your gift to me dad.
You said wings over roots.

The love in my heart,
The man by my side,
Is your blessing dad.
You didn't raise me to abide.

The me that I am,
The woman for the world to see,
Is cause; with unfathomable love baba,
You let me be ME.

Happiness

I met happiness today.
Well, ran into her really.
I was balancing my brown paper bag,
when a large Granny Smith Apple made a run for it.
I was getting ready to pick it up, perilously balanced
on my haunches; when happiness ran by.
Shyly picking it from the pavement, she extended her
chubby hands and gave me my apple.
And in meeting her clear brown eyes, her shy smile,
she left me with a lilting tune humming in my head.

I met happiness today.
He sat smoking.
Eyes crinkled and thin frame neatly arranged, at the
bus stop.
He tipped his cap at me, and said
"Have you seen such a clear blue sky, it's wonderful
to be old, so much time to just sit".
The bus came by.
"You first", I said,
"No, I will take the one at the end of my cigarette",
he smiled.
And I stepped into the bus, leaving all my daily cares
behind, with the old man's smile on my face.

1

I met happiness today.
He had nine tattoos etched on his face, arms and
neck.
I counted while in queue to pay my bill.
A serpent and musical notes collided under his chin
and disappeared into the neck of his orange t-shirt .
He sat on the pavement outside the shelter, and
carefully tore into exact halves a crusty looking bun.
The spotted mongrel by his side ate its share and
curled into him.
He munched his bit and scratched the pup behind its
ears.
The lady at the counter motioned to me,
and I stepped forward with a little tap-dance playing
in my ribcage.

It's real, that which they call happiness.
It doesn't have a calling card, nor is listed in the
phonebook.
You cannot get into your car and drive to its
residence.
But it is to be found wandering the streets,
and just where you were not looking,
You may run into it.

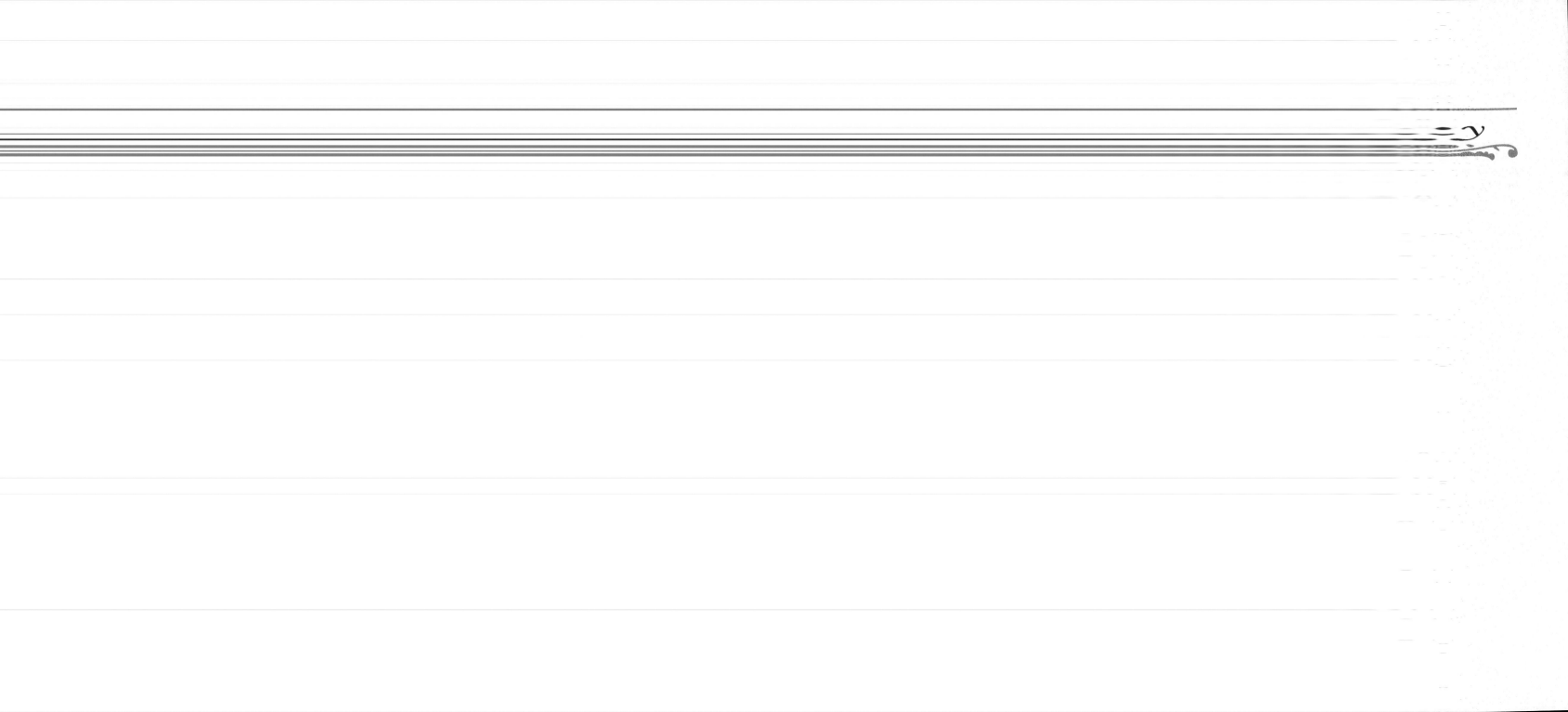

I thought of you
As birds huddle
With their youn
In night- dew en

I thought of you
As I do each nig
Blending my har
Into fragrant me
And slept in me

Nostalgia

Sunbeams filter through the drawn shades,
gently pushing dust mites into a frenzied dance.
A dark room, in ageless slumber, opens a
hesitating eye.
Memories of childhood, joys of an innocent youth.....
tumble in.

A dancing pattern of light and shadows mingle and
rush apart;
Tantalizing, awakening memories of yesteryears.
Delightful days, nuance- filled nights, tears and
giggles, fragments of a life well-lived.

Kaleidoscopic images, some in sepia some brushed in
vivid strokes,
Some tinged with sorrow, others loaded with regret
or bursting with joy.
Multi -faceted, multi -dimensional, seeped in emotions,
yet removed forever from any edits.

For the path can only be directed forward, and a
quick glance backwards is all yesterdays allow.
With a sigh, and a smile...life goes on.

Life

The autumn sun dipped.
Shadows were getting longer each day,
and darkness appeared a little earlier to gobble up
the sun,
like a monster with a belly full of hunger.

The little girl sat throwing and catching pebbles.
A lonely game in which she had a listless dog for
company.
All was still, not a rustle in the trees,
the very earth seemed to have slowed down.

Fires were starting to get lit and wispy smoke curled
up from chimneys,
Ghostly arms curling up agonizingly towards the
molten sky, yet the girl played on.
Chink of pebble against pebble, the only sound
breaking the silence,
as night continued to fall, in curtains of grey.

And in that evening light, half covered by a cloak,
curled up against a tree stump, sat Death.
Motionless yet with every sense alert,
staring with unwavering focus at the little girl
counting pebbles.

Clink against each clink it counted,
heartbeat against heartbeat
drumming against the little girl's chest.
the calm ebb and flow of untainted blood.

Unfettered dreams and unbridled hope
pulsating in steady rhythm in her heart.
Lub-a-dub, lub-a-dub
lulling death like a lullaby.

Death sat up stiffly, shaking off the soporific lull and
refocused on it's task.
This would not be a heavy load,
this wisp of a girl would fit just right under it's
cloak.
And just like that, would be gone like the last few rays
of that autumn sun.

The dog felt the presence, like all animals do.
Evolution had robbed man of that sixth sense,
which now lay buried so deep in Darwinian
adaptation,
as not to feel the brush of parallel universes.

But the dog stirred, and raised its head looking in the
direction of the stump,
the short hairs on its back rising, its slumber
forgotten
and it started to move back, on its haunches not
looking away, while it tried to soundlessly retreat
from this black energy which sucked away at life
and light.

And then it froze, arrested in its retreat.
As crystal- like laughter rang out from the child.
What had amused her is hard to say,
for who can question the heart of a child?

Her laugh rang out, pure and white,
and reached for the skies like thousand fireflies
bursting out from under heavy blades of grass.
And Death caught its breath.

In a throat which had never sucked air,
this breath of life punched like a physical blow.
Death fell back, in shock and awe,
just as her laughter pierced the sky and caught in its
resonance, the departing sun.

In a magical moment, a last sliver of light pierced
through the descending night and mirrored back her
laugh.
Death felt itself dissipate, washed away in this tidal
surge of life.
Melting back into the darkness, reduced to but a
fraction of itself.
Bewildered, stunned yet awestruck by something
beyond its comprehension.

The merry little girl gathered up her pebbles,
as they glinted like diamonds in the last light.
And as the first star peeped into the village,
she ran home into her mother's arm.

Game of life

My game is not with you,
Your life's not mine to lead,
I may walk with you,
But on my own two feet.

My dreams are mine alone.
My soul craves its own light.
While we may stop at the same stream,
My thirst's not quenched tonight.

So journey on I must,
while you may rest awhile,
for when the last star fades,
I must be my own light.

Calm

A few days I want to give you, of life and living.
A few feathers, to fly and soar in.
Cause in my mind's eye I see,
the person you might be, had the breeze not turned
into a squall.

I see you trudge in the eye of the storm, fighting to
walk on,
while the winds swirl around you, with hunched
shoulders you push on.
I want you to stop pushing, my friend.
Rest awhile, in the eye of the storm.

A few days I want to give you, of life and living,
A few feathers, to fly and soar in.
Cause in my mind's eye I see,
the person you might be, had the breeze not turned
into a squall.

Lost Chances

I buried that cry deep in my heart,
the angst which came from things I did not start.
The dreams I left by the roadside,
the paths I did not chart.

The love I did not claim,
the purple moon, Northern Lights,
the mountain not climbed,
for fear of heights.

The laugh suppressed, that strapless dress,
the weekend trip, the skinny dip.
The third helping, that sweet desert,
the last cocktail I did not sip.

The unopened letter, the word not said,
the scattered maybes I left in my stead.
and just like that, it's the end of the road
I turned a bend, and there I stood.

My life behind me, dreams trailing in time,
Clattering in the wind, like a broken wind- chime.
Was this it, did it all come to naught,
I closed my eyes and pushed hard at the thought.

Pushed it away with all my might,
till it rolled away into the night.
I took a right, with all I had left,
my dreams, my hopes and continued my quest.

Existential

You stand at the busy intersection,
waiting for the light to turn green and say WALK.
I stand next to you at the crossroads of life,
should I walk away?

Unplug the music from your ears,
can't you hear my cry for help?
Stop the damn foot-tapping,
be still for a while, while I take a breath.

Stop the humming, don't use up my oxygen,
There's just enough for the two of us.
Can you not see me standing next to you?
Fervently hoping the light stays red.

Chaos

Shiva danced his cosmic dance,
the heavens shook and the earth spewed fire.
From the belly of the earth was born,
chaos, as intrinsic as human desire.

The earth still spins and hearts beat on,
and thoughts move at a frenzied pace.
Words spew venom and minds conspire,
to create ripples in our mind- space.

Trapped we live under an open sky,
our joys all ours to claim.
Yet peace tap- dances an arms- length away,
while mankind decides on who to lay the blame.

Inner world

I woke up today, sat up in bed;
Reached out to pick my mobile and specs.
Then I stopped, slowly pulled back my hand;
Took a breath and gathered myself.

I was not ready to look out;
through the window to the world just yet.
Nor into the mobile world; we carry with us always.
Not just yet.

Let me take a minute to look into me-at I.
What does the temperature feel like ?
in the furnace of my soul;
in the coolness of my mind.

What are the headlines today?
in the blog of my thoughts;
in the banner of my reflections.

How is my inner world today?
Light? dark? hopeful? Lost?
Eager? meagre? cheeky? Somber?

In the stillness of a sublime dawn,
let me hear the steady beat of my heart-my friend
for life;
and know I am not alone,

For my world is within.
Let me dive into it and float a while;
in my inner pool, before I step into;
The world without.

On the Platform

All this time, there you sat,
looking at me through shaded eyes.

You said no word and yet your being,
welded to mine, seamlessly.

Your dreams I browsed, our thoughts combined,
fears and joys lay entwined.

The train arrived and you were gone,
I lifted my book and read on.

Seeds of Peace

What is peace? to each his own,
Yet all humanity reaps the fruit of a seed sown.

To a new mother, it is a night's deep sleep,
a pain free day, to the diseased.

To that emaciated little boy, living in the slums;
Peace is a day when hunger is satiated by crumbs.

To the battered and the victims of abuse;
Peace is freedom, the right to refuse.

Peace is not merely the lack of war,
Fought on shores, and lands afar.

It is intrinsic to every life;
Much closer home, than just absence of strife.

It's measured in the steady rhythm of each heart;
In smiles and tears that emotions impart.

In calm waters and rustling breeze;
You catch glimpses of it in an infant's deep sleep.

In snow-draped mountains, silent streams,
It's the sky at dawn, painted with rose-hued dreams.

man sow a tiny seed of peace;
way he knows best to make turmoil cease.

through their collective intent, one morn;
nity will awake to peace reborn.

The Endless Wait

The thin little boy, on his haunches sat;
Marking little crosses on the dry sandy earth.

A cross for each day and a line per month;
Intensely focused for all he was worth.

The dry scratch of twig on earth,
And a buzzing fly, was all he heard.

Shielding his eyes, he looked up at the skies,
A blinding white, not a cloud in sight.

The little boy sighed, fixed on the horizon his stare.
And wished with all his heart to see a cloud appear.

He was all of four and it had been a year,
Since his father left to bring glory, to whom was yet
unclear.

He will be back when the rains come,
Ma said he would return, to the beat of a victorious
drum.

Yet her voice was low and trembled just so;
And he wondered why baba had needed to go.

If only war and peace were his decisions to make;
There could be no guesses on the one he would take.

The Sound of Silence

I sat in a crowded room,
And switched off the noise.
Muted the sounds,
Shut down that voice.

"Look at us", it said,
Urgent and loud.
"There's none like us,
Align and be proud".

Seek to be accepted,
be part of the pack.
Wear our colours,
join our frat.

Rally around us,
pay abeyance to our queen.
Building the beehive,
must be your sole dream.

Dare you wear white,
when the rest of us wear pink.
Why're you lost in a book,
the sunny outdoors won't make you shrink.

Loud chatters, whispered gossips,
The why nots and why's.
Expectations, ramifications,
opinions and ploys.

This room is crowded,
Though I sit in your midst,
The noise bounces off me,
The mute button's in my fist.

The Me in Us

What is important- you, me or our togetherness?

The spatial width of the universe,
for us to roam alone and claim our souls.
Or the depth of our world as one,
to dive and discover.

The seeds we plant in our orchard, prune and wait to flower.
So we can smell the essence of us when our skin is weathered
in the autumn of our lives.
Or those we plant in our mind and soul,
nurture with books read, roads travelled and lives lived.

Does our US come in the way of you and me?
The held hands and entwined lives.
Buffering our singularity,
with "we", "us" and "ours".

Or does it polish our solitary vessels, with rubs and caresses,
till it shines brighter.
And retains more without splashes,
when securely held.

Love is a Verb

Your love, my Love; is not a noun.
It speaks a tongue yet without a sound.
In silence you stand, unwavering and still,
yet every pore of you resounds; with me, just me.
Through every action, and each tilt of head,
your eyes follow me around in your stead.

My deepest thoughts, most desperate dreams,
those long abandoned as mere fallacy.
You look them up and dust them down,
and hand to me like a gilt edged crown.
You own but a few hundred words;
or so I feel since you seldom sprout.

Yet in the depth of your fathomless eyes,
I suspect thousands of stories reside.
And in those stories there is but one tale,
Of You and me and countless lifetimes in detail.
Existences in today and in eons gone by,
Projections in futures yet unconceived.

Such is your love; my Love, for me,
it is the very air I breathe.

Joy

Joy is not that commodity being hawked at the
roadside shack,
like a bunch of gaily coloured gypsy scarves.
Or the mound of ocean-patterned shells,
the sun browned urchin is waving in your face.
But it comes close.

It is colourful, ornate, perhaps not worth more than
a few loose coins or a wrinkled note bunched and
lying forgotten in the left back pocket of your worn-
out jeans.
It is carefree, sun-kissed, in your face and irreverent.
Childlike and cheeky in its demand for your
attention,
seeking you part with a little bit of metal and plastic
in exchange for the elusive, wispy, ephemeral....a fair
trade if there was any.

For joy is best built by joining together randomly,
bits and pieces of inconsequential objects, emotions
and acts.
Gluing them together, or stringing them in gaily-
hued threads
and tilting your head to change your perspective.

Till you catch sight of that pattern only you can
decipher...and it makes you smile.

The Warrior's Prayer

Skies torn asunder by lightening,
a forbidding grey envelops the earth.
Yet know when you sit in silence,
the sun's shining on a distant turf.

There is joy immeasurable just beyond,
where you see just pain today.
And when the clouds part my dear one,
it will be one glorious day.

Life is lived in moments,
strung together by many a breath.
What today is heaped with torments,
will also die a natural death.

There will be sparking sunrises,
and dew-encrusted days.
Where today you lie in darkness.
will soon be infused with rays.

Get up my lonesome warrior,
and fight another day.
Knowing, from your angst,
is born strength to pave the way.

Little Lies

Those little lies you tell me,
you think they fade away.
Into the ether they vanish
like the sun's dipping ray.

But they stay and linger,
in the corners of my mind.
and start to burrow a little hole,
Not very easy to find.

You think it's done and dusted,
and these lies don't have a name.
But though they burrow deeply
nothing's just the same.

I look at you with wonder,
And try to find the trust.
But, darling in those little lies,
Our "us" has gathered rust.

Genesis of Hate

And they entered the dark alleys of the mind,
Narrow claustrophobic streets.
Closing in on both sides,
with the jagged edges,
of hastily constructed masonry.

Bricks of bigotry.
Stones of distrust.
Tiny, treacherous pebbles of discrimination,
that poked at their sides incessantly.

Scrapping raw wounds.
Creating gaping holes.
Through which the blood of,
Humanity seeped in a crimson stream.

Engulfed in darkness,
under a grey sky,
which rumbled threateningly.
They cowered and whimpered,
and in their terror huddled together,
Like a murder of crows, brought together only by their
fear.

Noisy, raucous, blistering mobs.
Born of darkness.
Trapped in the narrow maze of hate,
feeding off anything that is not black,
doesn't have sharp beaks and claws,
Anything that doesn't caw.

Born with wings.
Yet consigned to eternally tread grime.
In the dark alleys,
of their narrow mind.

In the face of Mortality

We come from a vast unknown,
and to the majestic oneness we return,
with a handful of breaths in between.
Souls in search of infinity.

We live in a rolling kaleidoscope,
of light and dark,
days and nights fused into one,
And call it a lifetime.

We search within and without,
for meaning and worth.
Waking each day with wonder anew,
Yet racing at breakneck speed, towards the finishing
line.

At times we pause,
borrow a drop from the ocean of time,
and yet the waves continue to pound,
upon the shores of eternity.

Mornings rise, twilight falls,
hearts beat and blood flows,
wrinkles gather, eyelids droop
hair turns grey, spines stoop.

And yet we rise, each new year,
to hold close those, that are dear.
And in each wispy, ethereal morn,
experience eternity, each day reborn.

Memories of You

The scribbles and doodles,
in the margins of my notebook.
Those fragments of my heart,
which you left in your stead.

The sepia- hued memories,
faded with handling.
That lipstick mark,
on one unwashed wine glass.

That laughter still ringing in my ear,
the strand of hair carefully preserved.
The scent of your perfume,
on perfect strangers in the subway.

The dog-eared book of corny couplets,
that single earring nestled in my armoire.
That ringtone set on autoplay,
the set of napkins folded into swans.

The white tulips which bloom each year,
the jasmine tea bags gathering dust.
The sunsets which go un-watched,
the yoga mat neatly curled in a corner.

The mauve lipstick in a forgotten nook,
those empty hangers in the cupboard.
The pastel towels by the sink,
The stack of post-its by the fridge.

They follow me like a shadow,
relentless, unyielding, attached.
As I continue to stumble through,
this land of the living.

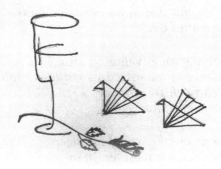

God

In the pores of oven-warm bread,
in the folds of sun-dried sheets,
in the blossoming of dew-encrusted buds,
I find hope and God.

In the calm of an enveloping dusk,
in the silence of majestic star-studded nights,
in the steady chitter of a cricket,
I glimpse peace and God.

In the rhythmic breath of my sleeping love,
in the crinkle of a toothless grin,
in the giggles of a carefree child,
I touch love and God.

In the writings of long gone poets,
in the chanting in unknown tongues,
in the brush- strokes of roadside artists,
I know faith and God

And that is all the God I wish to know.

In Sync

Did you walk today?
Placing the soles of your feet,
on the dew- laden bosom of the earth.

Did you touch the grass,
and feel your cells merge with the soil?
Did it exchange a forgotten language
in pulsating atoms of existence?

Did you wet your feet today,
in the flowing brooks of life?
Did it wash away your accumulated bits and bytes,
and fill the vacuum with the waters of life.

Dust we are,
air and dust held together by the fragile thread of a
million breaths.
Did you pause and take a breath today?

Present

If there were no tomorrows,
nor yesterdays to fall back on.
Would you know who you were today?

In this pinpoint of time,
bereft of dimensions,
of benchmarks and projections,
would you answer, if I called your name?

If you could not look
to left nor right.
If there was no forward or behind,
would you be fathomable in your today?

If the waves stopped in mid-tide,
and the birds in mid-flight,
would you dive deep within,
and soar high without?

Who are you when you awake each day?
Is it a mere collation of your had beens and will be's?
Or is there a YOU in there, waiting to break free,
to be, just me.

You

In you, I saw me.
Possibilities and dreams,
Hopes, fears, aspirations.
All my imperfect bits,
reflected in mirrored perfection.
And in knowing you;
I finally knew me.

Propensity for Joy

You have faced sorrow.
That heavy gnawing thing,
that has no name.

Which burrows into your insides,
and reaches recesses you didn't know existed.
It courses like acid,
creating pathways, pooling in inky puddles;
Invading and swamping.
Drawing on fragmented memories,
to heap on fresh pain.

It stupefies you, renders you immobile,
and makes your veins course with lead.
That black hole which swallows you whole,
and seems to have no bottom.
Yet is housed in that fistful of grey matter,
we call the mind.

And having housed sorrow,
do you not wonder, how much joy you can hold?

Seeds of Change

*You left me behind
an image, a memory.
You changed your mind,
and came back looking,
yet could not find.
The seed had sprouted wings
and flown away,
From the prison of your memories.*

ME TOO

2 words, a thousand stories,
bubbling up like molten, suppressed lava,
scorching, simmering gathering strength and voice.
And there are those silent voices too,
stifling their Me- Toos in shame, discomfort and the
need to not let the beast out.

A thousand voices, as many tales.
Across boundaries, ages, class and creed,
the beast preys.
On innocence who can't yet put a name to the
discomfort.
On teens struggling to isolate the incident from sense
of self and in failing, living with scarred psyches.
On women choosing to shrink their bodies into balls
of armour
in jostling buses, trains, elevators;
And lowering their gaze, turning away to severe eye
contact of salivating, goading beasts.

Homes are not cocoons, families not a stamp of
safety,
the beast stalks wherever there is vulnerability and
ease.
It is sly and cunning, and will not desist.
Neither garments that cover, nor education and
careers that empower, provides reprieve.
The beast stalks in boardrooms and drawing rooms
with equal stealth.

Leaving visible and invisible scars, drawing blood.
Some scars burn in the light of day.
Some fester and glow in the dark,
corroding souls, tainting minds, defiling bodies.
Eating into dreams, digging into hearts,
leaving gaping black holes in its trail.

Raise your voice, build your strength,
stand next to those who can't.
Emote, empathize, lend credence,
support, listen, act, mobilize.
Remove the shame, tear down the stigma.
And above all care.

Care to look deep into those you know and into
unknown eyes.
For every story told, there are a hundred stifled
silent cries of "Me Too".
For every past trauma recalled, tens are being
perpetrated each day.
Be the plug, stop the flow,
Not just, "ME TOO", say, "NO MORE".

Being ME

I am ecstatic to see,
there's only one ME.
Brimming with quirks and idiosyncrasy,
Wonderfully, uniquely me.

The world honks and tries to steer,
defines and slots, and judgments rear.
Tries to mold, arrange in a tidy fold,
to place in their pocket like a cigarette rolled.

Through it all, I sit amused,
sometimes frown, but mostly bemused.
Hack n chip at all you can see,
yet what remains will still be me.

And so it's true, for all of you,
just as special as a drop of dew.
Landed on earth, to quench a thirst,
and will be gone, at the end of morn.

Abundant is life and you are you,
to covet another's, is to sit and stew.
Live your life and set yourself free,
cause try as you might, you'll never be me.

Span of Life

And a day will come,
as it surely must.
When you will fit,
into a fistful of dust.

For today you can place
that thought into a deep recess,
of the mind's attic and refuse to see it.
Hoping by not acknowledging,
it will fade away into dust mites.

Today you will resent my words,
the mirror I hold before you,
forcing you to turn from your petty games,
and embrace the largess of life.
Nudging you to dilute your allegiances,
and embrace your people in their entirety.

Know that no meditation, God nor prayers,
will compare to open arms and openness of spirit.
It is but the span of your arms,
that will define the epitaph of your existence.

No, it should not dampen your zest for life,
nor is it melancholic to face this truth.
All it will lend to your days is the urgency,
of making it worth the breaths you took.

Thread of Hope

Remember those nights,
when you lay awake.
Tossing and turning,
all you hold dear at stake.

Digging desperately
through memory's archive,
for that one little thought,
that could bring respite.

Digging so deep
into a fathomless lair,
that you choked on your own thoughts,
couldn't come up for air.

The tunnels were deep,
more dirt piled up than you could sweep.
Mound after mound kept building up
yet frantically you dug, too petrified to give up.

And when you thought you couldn't cope,
a memory awoke, one sliver of hope.
And you clung to it with all your might,
Wanting to breathe, seeking some respite.

And such is life,
know this today.
Some times are joyous,
with every sorrow held at bay.

And then there are dark nights,
when you strain to see any lights.
Nights of raw despair,
of fretting and feeling the weight of care.

Yet in the midst,
of the highs and lows,
know there's always hope,
To soften the blows.

No man will live a hopeless life.
In small wonders he will find respite.
Such is the promise to all on earth born,
each night will be followed by a new dawn.

In The End

And that's all there is.
For in the end,
any Heaven or hell,
will all depend:
On who you touched,
in any small way,
as you wandered the earth,
Each new day.

When you lie down,
and take that last breath in;
It will not matter,
Did you lose or win.
You are your judge;
And you will know,
When the curtains close.
And you take your bow.